A FIERY FLYING ROLL

by
ABIEZER COPPE

Published by *The Rota* at the University of Exeter
1973

Printed in Great Britain
by Short Run Press Ltd, Exeter

BIBLIOGRAPHICAL NOTE

A fiery flying roll by Auxilium Patris, *alias* Abiezer Coppe (1619-72) appeared, both parts together, on 4 January 1649/50. Coppe, who had drifted during the 1640s into and out of presbyterianism and anabaptism, was at this time something of 'a ringleader' among the ranters, an amorphous group of sectarians. Confident that God had his being nowhere else but in all material things and creatures, ranters came in varying degrees to radicalism in politics and social issues, including, notoriously, sexual relations. Coppe himself deplored the mere 'sword-levelling' of Lilburne and the 'digging-levelling' of Winstanley, upon whose defeats at Burford and George's Hill, the ranters blazed into brief publicity (e.g., pp. 2, 4, 6). For Coppe God himself was 'that mighty Leveller ... comming (yea even at the doores) to Levell in good earnest, to Levell to some purpose, to Levell with a witnesse. ....' (p. 2). Coppe had heard all about it from a voice urging him to 'go up to *London*, to *London*, that great City, write write, write.' (*Preface*). *A fiery flying roll* is his response, setting out in vivid language a view of the intercourse between men and God as 'perfect freedome, and pure Libertinisme' (p. 1). These claims, coupled with Coppe's ecstatic behaviour, led to a Commons order of 1 February 1649/50 for searching out and destroying his tract (*C. J.* vi, p. 365; B. M., E. 669. f. 15(10)). The next two years saw a fierce pro- and anti-ranter campaign in the press, producing nearly 50 items. (See the list in A. L. Morton, *The world of the ranters* (London, 1970), pp. 113-14.) The act of 9 August 1650 (cap. 22; H. Scobell, *Acts and ordinances*, (London, 1657), pt. ii, pp. 124-6) for the punishment of 'atheistical, blasphemous and execrable opinions' was directed chiefly at ranters. On 11 July 1651, Coppe's *A return to the ways of truth* (B. M., E. 637. (4); Wing, C6090) withdrew some of his earlier opinions. Little is known of him in the next few years apart from a meeting with George Fox in 1655. At the Restoration Coppe settled as 'Dr Higham' in Surrey, where he practised physic, (like that other stranded radical, William Walwyn). He died in 1672, worn out, says Anthony Wood in a hostile account of this wayward Merton man, 'by certain infirmities which he had contracted in his rambles by drinking and whoring'. (*Athenae Oxonienses*, (London, 1691-2) ii, col. 367).

For a background to ranter theology see N. Cohn, *The pursuit of the millenium*, (London, 1957). A. L. Morton, *op. cit.*, is sympathetic and circumstantial. See also C. Hill, *The world turned upside down*, (London, 1972), chap. 10 and (a few apt comments) K. Thomas, *Religion and the decline of magic*, (London, 1971).

A fiery flying roll is reproduced by permission of the Trustees of the British Museum from the copy in the Thomason collection, E. 578. (13, 14), Wing, C6087. Wing, C6091, *A second fiery flying roule*, 1642, (B. M. only), is not a separate publication but E. 578. (14). The error presumably results from a misreading of the broken type in the 'date 1649' on the title page. There was only one printing of the tract. Wing, C6092 (B. M. only) is imaginary.

A Fiery Flying Roll:

A
Word from the Lord to all the Great Ones
of the Earth, whom this may concerne: Being the last WARNING PIECE at the dreadfull day of
JUDGEMENT.

For now the LORD is come
to
{ 1 *Informe* }
{ 2 *Advise and warne* }
{ 3 *Charge* }
{ 4 *Judge and sentence* }
the Great Ones.

As also most compassionately informing, and most lovingly and pathetically advising and warning *London*.

With a terrible Word, and fatall Blow from the LORD, upon the Gathered CHURCHES.

And all by his Most Excellent MAJESTY, dwelling in, and shining through
AUXILIUM PATRIS, alias, *Coppe*.

With another FLYING ROLL ensuing (to all the Inhabitants of the Earth.) The Contents of both following.

Isa. 23. 9, *The Lord of Hosts (is) staining the pride of all glory, and bringing into contempt all the honourable (persons and things) of the Earth.*
O London, London, how would I gather thee, as a hen gathereth her chickens under her wings, &c.
Know thou (in this thy day) the things that belong to thy Peace——
I know the blasphemy of them which say they are Jewes, and are not, but are the Synagogue of Satan, Rev. 2. 9. Jan. 4. 1649.

Imprinted at *London*, in the beginning of that notable day, wherein the secrets of all hearts are laid open; and wherein the worst and foulest of villanies, are discovered, under the best and fairest outsides. 1649.

The Preface.

An inlet into the Land of Promise, the new *Hierusalem*, and a gate into the ensuing Discourse, worthy of serious consideration.

Y Deare One.
All or None.
Every one under the Sunne.
Mine own.
My most Excellent Majesty (in me) hath strangely and variously transformed this forme.

And behold, by mine owne Almightinesse (In me) I have been changed in a moment, in the twinkling of an eye, at the sound of the Trump.

And now the Lord is descended from Heaven, with a shout, with the voyce of the Arch-angell, and with the Trump of God.

And the sea, the earth, yea all things are now giving up their dead. And all things that ever were, are, or shall be visible —— are the Grave wherein the King of Glory (the eternall, invisible Almightinesse, hath lain as it were) dead and buried.

But behold, behold, he is now risen with a witnesse, to save *Zion* with vengeance, or to confound and plague all things into himself; who by his mighty Angell is proclaiming (with a loud voyce) That Sin and Transgression is finished and ended; and everlasting righteousnesse brought in; and the everlasting Gospell preaching; Which everlasting Gospell is brought in with most terrible earth-quakes, and heaven-quakes, and with signes and wonders following. *Amen.* And

The Preface.

And it hath pleased my most Excellent Majesty, (who is universall love, and whose service is perfect freedome) to set this forme (the Writer of this Roll) as no small signe and wonder in fleshly *Israel*; as you may partly see in the ensuing Discourse.

And now (my deare ones!) every one under the Sun, I will onely point at the gate; thorow which I was led into that new City, new *Hierusalem*, and to the Spirits of just men, made perfect, and to God the Judge of all.

First, all my strength, my forces were utterly routed, my house I dwelt in fired; my father and mother forsook me, the wife of my bosome loathed me, mine old name was rotted, perished; and I was utterly plagued, consumed, damned, rammed, and sunke into nothing, into the bowels of the still Eternity (my mothers wombe) out of which I came naked, and whetherto I returned again naked. And lying a while there, rapt up in silence, at length (the body or outward forme being awake ll this while) I heard with my outward eare (to my apprehension) a most terrible thunder-clap, and after that a second. And upon the second thunder-clap, which was exceeding terrible, I saw a great body of light, like the light of the Sun, and red as fire, in the forme of a drum (as it were) whereupon with exceeding trembling and amazement on the flesh, and with joy unspeakable in the spirit, I clapt my hands, and cryed out, *Amen, Hale'ujah, Halelujah, Amen.* And so lay trembling, sweating, and smoaking (for the space of half an houre) at length with a loud voyce (I inwardly) cryed out, Lord, what wilt thou do with me; my most excellent majesty and eternall glory (in me) answered & sayd, Fear not, I will take thee up into mine everlasting Kingdom. But thou shalt (first) drink
a bitter

The Preface.

a bitter cup, a bitter cup, a bitter cup; whereupon (being filled with exceeding amazement) I was throwne into the belly of hell (and take what you can of it in these expressions, though the matter is beyond expression) I was among all the Devils in hell, even in their most hideous hew.

And under all this terrour, and amazement, there was a little spark of transcendent, transplendent, unspeakable glory, which survived, and sustained it self, triumphing, exulting, and exalting it self above all the Fiends. And confounding the very blacknesse of darknesse (you must take it in these tearmes, for it is infinitely beyond expression.) Vpon this the life was taken out of the body (for a season) and it was thus resembled, as if a man with a great brush dipt in whiting, should with one stroke wipe out, or sweep off a picture upon a wall, &c. after a while, breath and life was returned into the form againe; whereupon I saw various streames of light (in the night) which appeared to the outward eye; and immediately I saw three hearts (or three appearances) in the form of hearts, of exceeding brightnesse; and immediately an innumerable company of hearts, filling each corner of the room where I was. And methoughts there was variety and distinction, as if there had been severall hearts, and yet most strangely and unexpressibly complicated or folded up in unity. I clearely saw distinction, diversity, variety, and as clearly saw all swallowed up into unity. And it hath been my song many times since, within and without, unity, universality, universality, unity, Eternall Majesty, &c. And at this vision, a most strong, glorious voyce uttered these words, *The spirits of just men made perfect.* the spirits &c, with whom I had as absolute, cleare, full communion, and in a two fold more familiar

The Preface.

liar way, then ever I had outwardly with my dearest friends, and nearest relations. The visions and revelations of God, and the strong hand of eternall invisible almightinesse, was stretched out upon me, within me, for the space of foure dayes and nights, without intermission.

The time would faile if I would tell you all, but it is not the good will and pleasure of my most excellent Majesty in me, to declare any more (as yet) then thus much further: That amongst those various voyces that were then uttered within, these were some, *Blood, blood, Where, where?* upon the hypocriticall holy heart, &c. Another thus, *Vengeance, vengeance, vengeance, Plagues, plagues, upon the Inhabitants of the earth; Fire, fire, fire, Sword, sword,* &c. upon all that bow not down to eternall Majesty, universall love; I'le recover, recover, my wooll, my flax, my money. Declare, declare, feare thou not the faces of any; I am (in thee) a munition of Rocks, &c.

Go up to *London,* * to *London,* that great City, write, write, write. And behold I writ, and lo a hand was sent to me, and a roll of a book was therein, which this fleshly hand would have put wings to, before the time. Whereupon it was snatcht out of my hand, & the Roll thrust into my mouth; and I eat it up, and filled my bowels with it, (*Eze.*2.8. &c. *cha.*3.1,2,3.) where it was as bitter as worm-wood; and it lay broiling, and burning in my stomack, till I brought it forth in this forme.

And now I send it flying to thee, with my heart, And all

Per *AUXILIUM PATRIS*

* It not being shewen to me, what I should do, more then preach and print something, &c. very little expecting I should be so strangely acted, as to (my exceeding joy and delight) I have been, though to the utter cracking of my credit, and to the rotting of my old name which is damned, and cast out (as a toad to the dung-hill) that I might have a new name, with me, upon me, within me, which is, I am ———

The

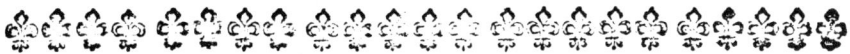

THE CONTENTS.

Chap. 1. Severall strange, yet true and seasonable informations to the great ones, as also an apologeticall hint of the Authors principle, &c.

Chap. 2. Severall new, strange, yet seasonable and good advice, and wholsome admonitions, and the last warning to the great ones, as from the Lord.

Chap. 3. Severall dismall, dolefull cryes, & out-cries, which pierce the eares and heart of his excellent Majesty, & how the King of Kings, the King of heaven charges the great ones of the earth.

Chap. 4. How the Judge of heaven and earth, who judgeth righteous judgment, passeth sentence against all those great ones, who like sturdy Oakes & tall Cedars wil not bow, and how he intends to breake them, and blow them up by the roots.

Chap. 5. A most compassionate information, and a most loving & patheticall warning and advice to London.

Chap. 6. A terrible word and fatall blow from the Lord upon the gathered Churches, who pretend most for God, yet defie the Almighty more then the vilest.

The second Flying Roll.

Chap. 1. The Authors commission to write. A terrible woe denounced against those that slight the roll. The Lords claim to all things; Together with a hint of a two-fold recovery, wherethrough the most hypocriticall heart shall be ripped up, &c.

Chap. 2. How the Lord will recover his outward things (things of this life) as money, corn, wool, flax, &c. and for whom: And how they shall be plagued that detaine them as their owne. Wherein also are some misticall hints concerning St. Michaels day, and the Lords day following it this yeare; as also of the dominicall letter D, &c.

Chap. 3. A strange, yet most true storie, under which is couch'd that lion, whose roaring shal make all the beasts of the field to tremble, and all the kingdomes of the world quake. Wherein also (in part) the subtilty of the welfavour'd harlot is discovered, and her flesh burnt with that fire which shall burn down all Churches, except that of the first borne, &c.

Chap. 4. That the Author hath been set as a sign and wonder, &c. as well as most of the Prophets formerly; as also what strange postures that divine Majestie (that dwels in his forme) hath set the'forme in: with the most strange and various effects thereof

upon

THE CONTENTS.

upon the spectators. His communion with the spirits of Just men made perfect, and with God the Judg of all hinted at.

CHAP. 5. The Authors strange and lofty carriage towards great ones, & his most lowly carriage towards beggars, rogues, prisoners, gypsies, &c. Together with a large Declaration What glory shall arise up from under all these ashes. The most strange & most secret and terrible, yet most glorious designe of God, in choosing base things, to confound things that are: And how, A most terrible viall poured out upon the Well-favoured harlot; and how the Lord is bringing into contempt not only honourable persons (with a vengeance) but all honourable holy things also.

Wholsome advice, with a terrible threat to the Formalists: And how BASE things have confounded base things: And how base things have been a fiery chariot to mount the Author up into divine glory and unspeakable Majestie: And how his wife is, & his life is in that beauty, which maketh visible beauty seem meere deformity.

CHAP. 6. Great ones must bow to the poorest peasants, or else they shall rue for it; No material sword or humane power (whatsoever) but the pure spirit of universall love, who is the eternall God, can breake the necke of tyranny, oppression, and abhominable pride and cruell murther, &c. A catalogue of severall Judgments recited, as so many warring-pieces to appropriators, impropriators, and anti-free communicants.

CHAP. 7. A farther discovery of the jubilee of the well favoured harlot, with a parley between her and the spirit. As also the horrid villany that lies hid under her smooth words, and sweet tongue (in pleading against the letter and history, and for the spirit and mistery, and all for her own ends) detected. Also upon what account the spirit is put, and upon what account the letter, &c. And what the true communion, and what the true breaking of bread is.

CHAP. 8. The wel-favoured harlots cloaths stript off, her nakednesse discovered, her nose slit. Her hunting after the young man void of understanding, from corner to corner, from religion to religion: And the spirit pursuing, overtaking, and destroying her, &c.

With a terrible thunder-clap i'th close.

A word from the Lord to all the Great Ones of the Earth (whom this may concerne) being the last Warning Piece, &c.

1 *The word of the Lord came expresly to me, saying, Sonne of man write a Roule, and these Words, from my mouth, to the Great ones, saying, thus saith the Lord:*
Slight not this Roule, neither laugh at it, least I slight you, and cause all men to slight and scorne you; least I destroy you, and laugh at your destruction, &c.
2 *This is, (and with a witnesse, some of you shall finde it, to be) an edg'd toole; and there's no jesting With it, or laughing at it.*
It's a sharp sword, sharpned, and also fourbished———
No sleepy Dormouse shall dare to creep up the edge of it.
Thus saith the Lord, You shall finde with a Witnesse, that I am now comming

to { 1 Informe
     2 Advise and Warne
     3 Charge
     4 Judge and sentence } you, O ye great ones.

CHAP. I.

Containing severall strange, yet true and seasonable Informations, to the great ones. As also an apologeticall hint, of the Authers Principle, standing in the front.———

1. Thus saith the Lord, *I inform you, that I overturn, overturn, overturn.* And as the Bishops, *Charles,* and the Lords, have had their turn, overturn, so your turn shall be next (ye surviving great ones) by what Name or Title soever dignified or distinguished) who ever you are, that oppose me, the Eternall God, who am UNIVERSALL Love, and whose service is perfect freedome, and pure Libertinisme.

* But

*An Apologeticall hint concerning the Authors Principle, the result--is negative; hee speaks little in the affirmative because not one in a hundred, yea even of his former acquaintance, now know him, neither must they yet.

2 * But afore I proceed any further, be it known to you, That although that excellent Majesty, which dwels in the Writer of this Roule, hath reconciled ALL THINGS to himselfe, yet this hand (which now writes) never drew sword, or shed one drop of any mans blood. [I am free from the blood of all men] though (I say) all things are reconciled to me, the eternall God (IN HIM) yet sword levelling, or digging-levelling, are neither of them his principle.

Both are as farre from his principle, as the East is from the West, or the Heavens from the Earth, (though, I say, reconciled to both, as to all things else) and though he hath more justice, righteousnesse, truth, and sincerity, shining in those low dunghils, (as they are esteemed) then in the Sunne, Moone, and all the Stars.

3 I come not forth (in him) either with materiall sword, or Mattock, but now (in this my day———) I make him my Swordbearer, to brandish the Sword of the Spirit, as he hath done severall dayes and nights together, thorow the streets of the great City.

4 And now thus saith the Lord:

Though you can as little endure the word LEVELLING, as could the late slaine or dead *Charles* (your forerunner, who is gone before you———) and had as live heare the Devill named, as heare of the Levellers (Men-Levellers) which is, and who (indeed) are but shadowes of most terrible, yet great and glorious good things to come.

5 Behold, behold, behold, I the eternall God, the Lord of Hosts, who am that mighty Leveller, am comming (yea even at the doores) to Levell in good earnest, to Leveil to some purpose, to Levell with a witnesse, to Levell the Hills with the Valleyes, and to lay the Mountaines low.

6 High Mountaines! lofty Cedars! its high time for you to enter into the Rocks, and to hide you in the dust, for feare of the Lord, and for the glory of his Majesty. For the lofty looks of man shall be humbled, and the haughtinesse of men shall be bowed downe, and the Lord ALONE shall be exalted in that day; For the day of the Lord of Hoasts, shall be upon every one that is proud, and lofty, and upon every one that is lifted up, and he shall be brought low. And upon all the Cedars of *Lebanon*, that

are

are high and lifted up, and upon all the Oaks of *Bashan*; and upon all the high Mountaines; and upon all the Hils that are lifted up, and upon every high Tower; and upon every fenced Wall; and upon all the Ships of *Tarshish*, and upon all pleasant Pictures.

And the LOFTINESSE of man shall be bowed down, and the haughtinesse of men shall be laid low. And the Lord ALONE shall be exalted in that day, and the Idols he shall utterly abolish.

And they shall go into the holes of the Rocks, and into the Caves of the Earth, for feare of the Lord, and for the glory of his Majesty, when he ariseth to shake terribly the earth.

In that day a man shall cast his Idols of Silver, and Idols of Gold —— to the bats, and to the Moles. To go into the Clefts of the Rocks and into the tops of the ragged Rocks, for feare of the Lord, and for the glory of his Majesty. For the Lord is now RISEN to shake terribly the Earth, *Isa.*2.10. to the end of the Chapter.

7 Hils! Mountains! Cedars! Mighty men! Your breath is in your nostrils.

Those that have admired, adored, idolized, magnified, set you up, fought for you, ventured goods, and good name; limbe and life for you, shall ceafe from you.

You shall not (at all be accounted of (not one of you) ye sturdy Oake) who bowe not downe before eternall Majesty: Vniversall Love, whose service is perfect freedome, and who hath put down the mighty (remember, remember your fore-runner) and who is putting down the mighty from their seats; and exalting them of low degree.

8 Oh let not, (for your owne sakes) let not the mother of Harlots in you, who is very subtle of heart.

Nor the Beast (without you) what do you call 'em? The Ministers, fat parsons, Vicars, Lecturers, &c. who (for their owne base ends, to maintaine their pride, and pompe, and to fill their owne paunches, and purses) have been the chiefe instruments of all those horrid abominations, hellish, cruell, devilish persecutions, in this Nation which cry for vengeance. For your owne sakes (I say) let neither the one, nor the other bewitch you, or charme your cares, to heare them say, these things shall not befall

Iſay 2:

you, theſe Scriptures ſhall not be fulfilled upon you, but upon the Pope, Turke, and Heathen Princes, &c.

9 Or if any of them ſhould (through ſubtilty for their owne baſe ends) creep into the Myſtery of that forementioned * Scripture.

And tell you, Thoſe words are to be taken in the Myſtery only; and they onely point out a ſpirituall, inward levelling (once more, for your owne ſakes, I ſay) believe them not.

10 'Tis true, the Hiſtory, or Letter, (I ſpeake comparatively) is but as it were haire-cloth; the Myſtery is fine Flax. My flix, ſaith the Lord, and the Thief and the Robber will ſteale from me my flix, to cover his nakedneſſe, that his filthineſſe may not appeare.

But behold, I am (now) recovering my flix out of his hand, and diſcovering his lewdneſſe——*verbum ſat*——

11 'Tis true, the Myſtery is my joy, my delight, my life.

And the Prime levelling, is laying low the Mountaines, and levelling the Hils in man.

But this is not all.

For lo I come (ſaith the Lord) with a vengeance, to levell alſo your Honour, Riches, &c. to ſtaine the pride of all your glory, and to bring into contempt all the Honourable (both perſons and things) upon the earth, Iſa. 23. 9.

12 For this Honour, Nobility, Gentility, Propriety, Superfluity, &c. hath (without contradiction) been the Father of helliſh horrid pride, arrogance, haughtineſſe, loftineſſe, murder, malice, of all manner of wickedneſſe and impiety; yea the cauſe of all the blood that ever hath been ſhed, from the blood of righteous *Abell*, to the blood of the laſt Levellers that were ſhot to death. *And now (as I live ſaith the Lord) I am come to make inquiſition for blood; for murder and pride, &c.*

13 I ſee the root of it all *The Axe is laid to the root of the Tree* (by the Eternall God, *My Self*, ſaith the Lord) *I will hew it down*. And as I live, I will plague your Honour, Pompe, Greatneſſe, Superfluity, and confound it into parity, equality, community; that the neck of horrid pride, murder, malice, and tyranny, &c. may be chopt off at one blow. And that my ſelfe, the Eternall God, who am Vniverſall Love, may fill the Earth with univerſall love, univerſall peace, and perfect freedome; which

can never be by humane sword or strength accomplished.

14 Wherefore bow downe, bow downe, you sturdy Oakes, and tall Cedars; bow, or by my self Ile break you.

Ile cause some of you (on whom I have compassion) to bow &c. and will terribly plague the rest.

My little finger shall be heavier on them, then my whole loynes were on *Pharaoh* of old.

15 And maugre the subtilty, and sedulity, the craft and cruelty of hell, and earth: this Levelling shall up.

Not by sword; we (holily) scorne to fight for any thing; we had as live be dead drunk every day of the weeke, and lye with whores i'th market place, and account these as good actions as taking the poore abused, enslaved ploughmans money from him (who is almost every where undone, and squeezed to death; and not so much as that plaguy, unsupportable, hellish burden, and oppression, of Tythes taken off his shoulders, notwithstanding all his honesty, fidelity, Taxes, Free quarter, petitioning &c. for the same,) we had rather starve, I say, then take away his money from him, for killing of men.

Nay, if we might have Captains pay, and a good fat Parsonage or two besides, we would scorne to be swordsmen, or fight with those (mostly) carnall weapons, for any thing, or against any one, or for our livings.

16 No, no, wee'll live in despite of our foes; and this levelling (to thy torment, O mighty man) shall up; not by sword, not by might, &c. but by my Spirit, saith the Lord.

For I am risen, for I am risen, for I am risen, to shake terribly the earth, and not the earth onely, but the heavens also, &c.

But here I shall cease informing you.

You may for your further information (if you please) reade my Route to all the rich Inhabitants of the earth.

Reade it if you be wife, I shall now advice you.

CHAP.

CHAP. II.

Containing severall new, strange, yet seasonable Admonitions, and good advice; as the last warning to the Great Ones of the Earth. from the Lord.

* Serò sapiunt
Pxryges, sed
nunquam Sera
est ad Bonos
mores via.

1 Admonition
to great ones.

1 Thus saith the Lord: Be * wise now therefore, O ye Rulers, &c. Be instructed, &c. Kisse the Sunne, &c. Yea, kisse Beggers, Prisoners, warme them, feed them, cloathe them, money them, relieve them, release them, take them into your houses, don't serve them as dogs, without doore. &c.

Owne them, they are flesh of your flesh, your owne brethren, your owne Sisters, every whit as good (and if I should stand in competition with you) in some degrees better then your selves.

2 Once more, I say, own them; they are your self, make them one with you, or else go howling into hell; howle for the miseries that are comming upon you, howle.

The very shadow of levelling, sword-levelling, man-levelling, frighted you, (and who, like your selves, can blame you, because it shook your Kingdome?) but now the substantiality of levelling is coming.

The Eternall God, the mighty Leveller is comming, yea come, even at the doore; and what will you do in that day.

Repent, repent, repent, Bow down, bow down, bow, or howle, resigne, or be damned; Bow downe, bow downe, you sturdy Oakes, and Cedars, bow downe.

Veile too, and kisse the meaner shrubs. Bow, or else (by my self saith the Lord) Ile breake you in pieces (some of you) others I will teare up by the roots; I will suddenly deale with you all, some in one way; some in another. Wherefore

  Each Begger that you meet
  Fall down before him, kisse him in the street.

Once more, he is thy brother, thy fellow, flesh of thy flesh.

Turne not away thine eyes from thine owne FLESH, least I pull out thine eyes, and throw thee headlong into hell.

3 Mine eares are fill'd brim full with cryes of poore prisoners, Newgate, Ludgate cryes (of late) are seldome out of mine eares.

Those

Those dolefull cryes, Bread, bread, bread for the Lords sake, pierce mine eares, and heart, I can no longer forbeare.

Wherefore high you apace to all prisons in the Kingdome,   *2 Admonition to great ones.*

4 Bow before those poore, nasty, lousie, ragged wretches, say to them, your humble servants, Sirs, (without a complement) we let you go free, and serve you, &c.

Do this (or as I live saith the Lord) thine eyes (at least) shall be boared out, and thou carried captive into a strange Land.

5 Give over, give over, thy odious, nasty, abominable fasting,   *3 Admonition to great ones* for strife and debate, and to smite with the fist of wickednesse. And instead thereof, loose the bands of wickednesse, undo the heavy burdens, let the oppressed go free, and breake every yoake. Deale thy bread to the hungry, and bring the poore that are cast out (both of houses and Synagogues) to thy house. Cover the naked: Hide not thy self from thine owne flesh, from a creeple, a rogue, a begger, he's thine owne flesh. From a Whoremonger, a thief, &c. he's flesh of thy flesh, and his theft, and wheredome is flesh of thy flesh also, thine owne flesh. Thou mayst have ten times more of each within thee, then he that acts outwardly in either, Remember, turn not away thine eyes from thine OWN FLESH.

6 Give over, give over thy midnight mischief.   *4 Admonition to great ones*
Let branding with the letter B. alone.

Be no longer so horridly, hellishly, impudently, arrogantly, wicked, as to judge what is sinne, what not, what evill, and what not, what blasphemy, and what not.

For, thou and all thy reverend Divines, so called (who Divine for Tythes, hire, and money, and serve the Lord Jesus Christ for their owne bellyes) are ignorant of this one thing.

7 That sinne and transgression is finisht, its a meere riddle, that they, with all their humane learning can never reade.

Neither can thy understand what pure honour is wrapt up in the Kings Motto, *Honi Soit qui Mal. y. Pense.* Evill to him that evill thinks.

Some there are (who are accounted the off scouring of all things) who are Noble Knights of the Garter. Since which——they could see no evill, thinke no evill, doe no evill, know no evill.

ALL is Religion that they speak, and honour that they do.

But

But all you that eat of the Tree of Knowledge of Good and Evill, and have not your Evill eye Pickt out, you call Good Evill, and Evill Good; Light Darknesse, and Darknesse Light; Truth Blasphemy, and Blasphemy Truth.

And you are at this time of your Father the Devill, and of your brother the Pharisee, who still say of Christ (who is now alive) say we not well that he hath a Devill.

9 Take heed, take heed, take heed.

Filthy blinde Sodomites called Angels men, they seeing no further then the formes of men.

10 There are Angels (now) come downe from Heaven, in the shapes and formes of men, who are full of the vengeance of the Lord; and are to poure out the plagues of God upon the Earth, and to torment the Inhabitants thereof.

Some of these Angels I have been acquainted withall.

And I have looked upon them as Devils, accounting them Devils incarnate, and have run from place to place, to hide my self from them, shunning their company; and have been utterly ashamed when I have been seen with them.

But for my labour; I have been plagued and tormented beyond expression. So that now I had rather behold one of these Angels * pouring out the plagues of God, cursing; and teaching others to curse bitterly.

*Rev. 15, Judges 5, Revel. 10, Neh.13.25,

And had rather heare a mighty Angell (in man) swearing a full-mouthd Oath; and see the spirit of *Nehemiah* (in any form of man, or woman) running upon an uncleane Jew (a pretended Saint) and tearing the haire of his head like a mad man, cursing, and making others fall a swearing, then heare a zealous Presbyterian, Independent, or * spirituall Notionist, pray, preach, or exercise.

* This will come in request with you next; you may remember that Independency, which is now so hug'd, was counted blasphemy, and banishment was too good for it.

11 Well! To the pure all things are pure. God hath so cleared cursing, swearing, in some, that that which goes for swearing and cursing in them, is more glorious then praying and preaching in others.

And what God hath cleansed, call not thou uncleane.

And if *Peter* prove a great transgressor of the Law, by doing that which was as odious as killing a man; if he at length (though he be loath at first) eat that which was common and uncleen &c. (I give but a hint) blame him not, much lesse lift up a finger

against

against, or plant a hellish Ordinance ——— against him, least thou be plagu'd, and damned too, for thy zeale, blinde Religion, and fleshly holinesse, which now stinks above ground, though formerly it had a good favour,

12 But O thou holy, zealous, devout, righteous, religious one (whoever thou art) that seest evill, or any thing uncleane; do thou sweare, if thou darest, if it be but (I'faith) I'le throw thee to Hell for it (saith the Lord) and laugh at thy destruction.

While Angels (in the forme of men) shall sweare, Heart, Blood, Wounds, and by the Eternall God, &c. in profound purity, and in high Honour, and Majesty.

13 Well! one hint more; there's swearing ignorantly, i'th darke, vainely, and there's swearing i'th light, gloriously.

Well! man of the earth! Lord *Esau*! what hast thou to do with those who sweare upon the former account?

Vengeance is mine, Judgement, Hell, Wrath, &c. all is mine (saith the Lord) dare not thou to set thy foot so impudently and arrogantly upon one step of my Throne: I am Judge my self—— Be wise, give over, have done———

14 And as for the latter sort of swearing, thou knowest it not when thou hearest it. It's no new thing for thee to call Christ Beel-zebub, and Beel-zebub Christ; to call a holy Angell a Devill, and a Devill an Angell.

15 I charge thee (in the name of the Eternall God) meddle not with either, let the Tares alone, least thou pull up the Wheat also, woe be to thee if thou dost. Let both alone (I say) least thou shouldest happen of a holy swearing Angell, and take a Lion by the paw to thine owne destruction.

Never was there such a time since the world stood, as now is.

Thou knowest not the strange appearances of the Lord, now a daies. Take heed, know thou hast been warned.

16 And whatever thou dost, dip not thy little finger in blood *Admonition* any more, thou art up to the elbowes already: Much sope, yea to great ones much nitre cannot cleanse thee, &c.

Much more have I to say to thee (saith the Lord) but I will do it secretly; and dart a quiver full of arrowes into thy heart; and I will now charge thee.

C   CHAP.

CHAP. III.

Containing severall dismall, dolefull cryes, and outcries, which pierce the eares and heart of his Excellent Majesty, the King of Kings. And how the King of Heaven chargeth the Great Ones of the Earth.

1 Thus saith the Lord, Be silent, O all flesh, before the Lord; be silent; O lofty, haughty, great ones of the Earth.
 There are so many Bils of Indictment preferred againſt thee, that both heaven and earth bluſh thereat.
 How long ſhall I heare the ſighs and groanes, and ſee the teares of poore widowes; and heare curſes in every corner; and all ſorts of people crying out oppreſſion, oppreſſion, tyranny, tyranny, the worſt of tyranny, unheard of, unnaturall tyranny.
 ——O my back, my ſhoulders. O Tythes, Excize, Taxes, Pollings, &c. O Lord! O Lord God Almighty!
 What, a little finger heavier then former loynes?
 What have I engaged my goods, my life, &c. forſooke my deareſt relations, and all for liberty and true freedome, for freedome from oppreſſion, and more laid on my back, &c.
 2 Mine eares are filled brim full with confuſed noiſe, cries, and outcries; O the innumerable complaints and groanes that pierce my heart (thorow and thorow) O aſtoniſhing complaints.
 Was ever the like ingratitude heard of ſince the world ſtood? what! beſt friends, fureſt friends, ſlighted, ſcorned, and that which cometh from them (in the baſeſt manner) contemned, and ſome rewarded with priſons, ſome with death?
 O the abominable perfidiouſneſſe, falſeheartedneſſe; ſelf-ſeeking, ſelf-inriching, and Kingdome-depopulating, and devaſtating, &c.
 Theſe, and divers of the ſame nature, are the cries of *England*. And can I any longer forbeare?
 I have heard, I have heard, the groaning of my people. And now I come to deliver them, ſaith the Lord.

Woe be to *Pharaoh* King of *Egypt*.

You Great Ones that are not tackt nor tainted, you may laugh and sing, when this hitteth it hitteth. And it shall hit home.

And this which followeth, all whom it concerneth, by what name or title soever dignified or distinguished.

3 You mostly hate those (called Levellers) who (for ought you know) acted as they did, out of the sincerity, simplicity, and fidelity of their hearts; fearing least they should come under the notion of Covenant-breakers, if they did not so act.

Which if so, then were they most barbarously, unnaturally, hellishly murdered; and they died Martyrs for God and their Countrey.

And their blood cries vengeance, vengeance, in mine ears, saith the Lord.

4 Well! let it be how it will; these * Levellers (so called) you mostly hated, though in outward declarations you owned their Tenents as your owne Principle.

So you mostly hate me (saith the Lord) though in outward declarations you professe me, and seeme to owne me, more then a thousand whom you despise, and account worse than your selves, who are nearer the Kingdome of Heaven then your selve.

You have killed Levellers (so called) you also (with wicked hand) have slain me the Lord of life, who am now risen, and risen indeed, (and you shall know, and feele it with a witnesse) to Levell you in good earnest. And to lay low all high hils, and every mountaine that is high, and lifted up, &c.

* Once more know, that Sword-leveling is not my principle; I onely pronounce the righteous judgements of the Lord upon Earth, as I durst.

5 Well! once more, read *Jam.* 5, 1. to 7 ——— Ye have killed the just ——— Ye have killed, ye have killed, ye have killed the just.

The blood cryeth in mine eares, Vengeance, vengeance, vengeance, vengeance is mine, I will recompence.

Well! what will you do with *Bray*, and the poore prisoners elsewhere? You know not what you do.

You little know what will become of you.

One of you had best remember your dream about your Fathers Moule———

6 Neither do I forget the one hundred spent in superfluous dishes (at your late great *London* Feast, for I know what———) when

when hundreds of poore wretches dyed with hunger.

I have heard a found in mine eares, that no leſſe then a hundred died in one week, pined, and ſtarved with hunger.

Howle you great ones, for all that feaſt daies dole, &c. heare your doome.

CHAP. IV.

How the Judge of Heaven and Earth, who judgeth righteous judgement, paſſeth ſentence againſt all thoſe Great Ones, who (like Oakes and tall Cedars) will not bow. And how he intends to blow them up by the roots.

1 Thus ſaith the Lord: All you tall Cedars, and ſturdy Oakes, who bow not down, who bow not down——
This ſentence is gone out of my mouth againſt you, MENE, MENE, TEKEL.

Thou art weighed in the ballances, and art found wanting.

God hath numbred thy Kingdome, and finiſhed it.

And thou, and all that joyne with thee, or are (in the leaſt degree) acceſſary to thy former, or like intended pranks, ſhall moſt terribly and moſt ſtrangely be plagued.

2 There is a little ſparke lies under (that huge heap of aſhes) all thine honour, pomp, pride, wealth, and riches, which ſhall utterly conſume all that is uppermoſt, as it is written.

The Lord, the Lord of Hoſts, ſhall ſend among his fat ones, leanneſſe; and under his glory he ſhall kindle a burning, like the burning of a fire, and the light of *Iſrael* ſhall be for a fire, and his holy one for a flame, and it ſhall burne and devoure his thornes, and his briers in one day.

And ſhall conſume the glory of his Forreſt, and of his fruitfull field, both ſoule and body (*i.e.* this ſhall be done inwardly and outwardly, and ſhall be fulfilled both in the hiſtory and myſtery) and the reſt of the trees of his Forreſt ſhall be few, that a childe may write them.

And the Lord, the Lord of Hoaſts, ſhall lop the bough with terror, and the high ones of ſtature ſhall be hewen down, and
the

haughty shall be humbled, And he shall cut down the thickets of the Forrest with iron, and *Lebanon* shall fall by a mighty one, *Isa.* 10.

3 Behold, behold, I have told you.

Take it to heart, else you'l repent every veine of your heart.

For your own sakes take heed.

Its my last warning.

For the cryes of the poore, for the oppression of the needy. For the horrid insolency of proud man, who will dare to sit in my throne, and judge unrighteous judgement.

Who will dare to touch mine Annoynted, and do my Prophets harme.

For these things sake (now) am I arrisen, saith the Lord,

In Auxilium Patris

CHAP. V.

1 O *London, London,* my bowels are rolled together (in me) for thee, and my compassions within me, are kindled towards thee.

And now I onely tell thee, that it was not in vaine that this forme ha h been brought so farre to thee, to proclaime the day of the Lord throughout thy streets, day and night, for twelve or thirteen dayes together.

And that I have been made such a signe, and a wonder before many of thine Inhabitants faces.

2 Many of them (among other strange exploits) beholding me, fall down flat at the feet of creeples, beggers, lazars, kissing their feet, and resigning up my money to them; being severall times over-emptied of money, that I have not had one penny left, and yet have recruited againe——

3 And now my hearts! you have been forwardly in all the appearances of God,

There is a strange one (now on foot) judge it not, least you be judged with a vengeance.

4 Turne not away your eyes from it, least you (to your torment) heare this voyce——*I was a Stranger, and ye tooke me not in.*

Well,

Well I bow down before Eternall Majesty, who is universall love, bow down to equality, or free community, that no more of your blood be spilt; that pride, arrogance, covetuousnesse, malice, hypocrisie, self-seeking, &c. may live no longer. Else I tremble at whats comming upon you.

Remember you have been warned with a witnesse.

Deare hearts Farewell.

CHAP. VI.

A terrible word, and fatall blow from the Lord, upon the gathered Churches (so called) especially upon those that are stiled Anabaptists.

1. HE that hath an eare to heare, let him hear what the Spirit saith against the Churches.

* The house of vanity.
* The house of God.

Thus saith the Lord: Woe be to thee * *Bethaven*, who callest thy selfe by the name * *Bethel*, it shall be more tollerable (now in the day of judgement, for *Tyre* and *Sydon*, for those whom thou accountest, and callest Heathens, then for thee.

2 And thou proud *Lucifer*, who exaltest thy self above all the Stars of God in heaven, shalt be brought down into hell; it shall be more tollerable for *Sodom* and *Gomorrah*, for drunkards and whoremongers, then for thee. Publicans and Harlots shall, Publicans and Harlots do sooner enter into the Kingdome of Heaven, then you.

I'le give thee this fatall blow, and leave thee.

3 Thou hast affronted, and defied the Almighty, more then the vilest of men (upon the face of the earth) and that so much the more, by how much the more thou takest upon thee the name of Saint, and assumest it to thy self onely, damning all those that are not of thy S.ct.

4 Wherefore be it knowne to all Tongues, Kinreds, Nations, and languages upon earth, That my most Excellent Majesty, the King of glory, the Eternall God, who dwelleth in the forme of the Writer of this Roll (among many other strange and great exploits) hath i'th open streets, with his hand fiercely stretcht out, his hat cockt up, his eyes set as if they would sparkle out; and with

a mighty

a mighty loud voyce charged 100. of Coaches, 100. of men and women of the greater ranke, and many notorious, deboist, swearing, royftering roaring Cavalliers (so called) and other wilde sparks of the Gentry: And have proclaimed the notable day of the Lord to them, and that through the streets of the great Citie, and in Southwark; Many times great multitudes following him up and down, and this for the space of 12. or 13. dayes: And yet (all this while) not one of them lifting up one finger, not touching one haire of his head, or laying one hand on his raiment.

But many, yea many notorious vile ones, in the esteeme of men (yea of great quality among men) trembling and bowing to the God of heaven, &c.

But when I came to proclaim (also) the great day of the Lord (among you) O ye carnall Gospellers.

The Devill (in you) roared out, who was tormented to some purpose, though not before his time.

He there shewed both his phangs and pawes, and would have torn me to pieces, and have eaten me up. Thy pride, envy, malice, arrogance, &c. was powred out like a river of Brimstone, crying out, a Blasphemer, a Blasphemer, away with him: At length threatning me, and being at last raving mad, some tooke hold of my Cloak on one side, some on another, endeavouring to throw me from the place where I stood (to proclaime his Majesties message) making a great uproar in a great congregation of people: Till at length I wrapt up my self in silence (for a season) for the welfavour'd harlots confusion, &c.

And to thine eternall shame and damnation (O mother of witchcrafts, who dwelleft in gathered Churches) let this be told abroad: And let her FLESH be burnt with FIRE.

Amen, Hallelujah.

FINIS.

A SECOND
Fiery Flying Roule:

TO
All the Inhabitants of the earth; specially to the rich ones.

OR,

A sharp sickle, thrust in, to gather the clusters of the vines of the earth, because her grapes are (*now*) fully ripe. And the great, notable, terrible, (yet glorious and joyfull) day of the LORD is come; even the Day of the Lords Recovery and Discovery. Wherein the secrets of all hearts are ripped up; and the secret villanies of the holy Whore, the well-favoured Harlot (who scornes carnall Ordinances, and is mounted up into the notion of Spiritualls) is discovered: And even her flesh burning with unquenchable fire. And the pride of all glory staining.

Together with a narration of various, strange, yet true stories: And severall secret mysteries, and mysterious secrets, which never were afore written or printed.

As also, That most strange Appearance of eternall Wisdome, and unlimited Almightinesse, in choosing base things: And why, and how he chooseth them. And how (most miraculously) they (even base things) have been, are, and shall be made fiery Chariots, to mount up some into divine glory, and unspotted beauty and majesty. And the glory that ariseth up from under them is confounding both Heaven and Earth. With a word (by way of preface) dropping in as an in-let to the new Hierusalem.

These being some things of what are experimented.

Per AUXILIUM PATRIS כה

Howle, rich men, for the miseries that are (just now) coming upon you, the rust of your silver is rising up in judgment against you, burning your flesh like fire, &c.

And now I am come to recover my corn, my wooll, and my flax, which thou hast (theevishly and hoggishly) detained from me, the Lord God Almighty, in the poore and needy.

Also howle thou holy Whore, thou well-favour'd Harlot: for God, and I, have chosen base things to confound thee, and things that are.

And the secrets of all hearts are now revealing by my Gospell, who am a stranger, and besides my selfe, to God, for your sakes. Wherefore receive me, &c. els expect that dismall doom, Depart from me ye cursed, I was a stranger, and ye took me not in.

Printed in the Yeer 1649.

Chap. I.

The Authors Commission to write, a terrible wo denounced against those that slight the Roule. The Lords claime to all things; together with a hint of a two-fold recovery, wherethrough the most hypocriticall heart shall be ript up.

1. THe Word of the Lord came expressely to me, saying, write, write, write.

2. And ONE stood by me, and pronounced all these words to me with his mouth, and I wrote them with ink in this paper.

3. Wherefore in the Name and Power of the eternall God, I charge thee burn it not, tear it not, for if thou dost, I will tear thee to peices (saith the Lord) and none shall be able to deliver thee; for (as I live) it is the day of my vengeance.

4. Read it through, and laugh not at it; if thou dost I'l destroy thee, and laugh at thy destruction.

5. Thus saith the Lord, though I have been a great while in coming, yet I am now come to recover my corn, and my wool, and my flax, &c. and to discover thy lewdnesse, *Hos.* 2.

Thou art cursed with a curse, for thou hast robbed me (saith the Lord) of my corn, my wool, my flax, &c. Thou hast robbed me of my Tythes, for the Tythes are mine, *Mal.* 3. And the beasts on a thousand hills, yea all thy baggs of money, hayricks, horses, yea all that thou callest thine own are mine.

6. And now I am come to recover them all at thy hands, saith the Lord, for it is the day of my recovery, and the day of my discovery, &c. And there is a two-fold recovery of two sorts of things; inward, and outward, or civil, and religious, and through both, a grand discovery of the secrets of the most hypocriticall heart, and a ripping up of the bowels of the welfavoured Harlot, the holy Whore, who scorns that which is called prophanesse, wickednesse, loosenesse, or libertinisme, and yet her self is the mother of witchcrafts, and of all the abominations of the earth.

But more of this hereafter.

7. For the present, I say, Thus saith the Lord, I am come to recover all my outward, or civill rights, or goods, which thou callest thine own.

Chap. II.

How the Lord will recover his outward things [things of this life] as Money, Corn, &c. and for whom, and how they shall be plagued who detaine them as their owne. VVherein also are some mysticall hints concerning Michaelmasse day, and the Lords day following it this year, as also of the Dominicall letter D. this year.

1. And the way that I will walk in (in this great notable and terrible day of the Lord) shall be thus, I will either (strangely & terribly, to thy torment) inwardly, or els (in a way that I will not acquaint thee with) outwardly, demand all mine, and will say on this wise.

2. Thou hast many baggs of money, and behold now I come as a thief in the night, with my sword drawn in my hand, and like a thief as I am, ---- I say deliver your purse, deliver sirrah! deliver or I'l cut thy throat!

3. Deliver MY money to such as * poor despised *Maul* of Dedington in Oxonshire, whom some devills incarnate (insolently and proudly, in way of disdaine) cry up for a fool, some for a knave, and mad-man, some for an idle fellow, and base rogue, and some (true lier then they are aware of) cry up for a Prophet, and some arrant fools (though exceeding wise) cry up for more knave then foole, &c. when as indeed, ther's pure royall blood runs through his veins, and he's no lesse then a Kings Son, though not one of you who are devills incarnate; & have your eyes blinded with the God of this world, know it.

* For some speciall reason this poor wretch is here instanced.

4. I say (once more) deliver, deliver, my money which thou hast to him, and to poor creeples, lazars, yea to rogues, thieves, whores, and cut-purses, who are flesh of thy flesh, and every whit as good as thy self in mine eye, who are ready to starve in plaguy Goals, and nasty dungeons, or els by my selfe, saith the Lord, I will torment thee day and night, inwardly, or outwardly, or both waies, my little finger shall shortly be heavi-

er on thee, especially on thee thou holy, righteous, religious *Appropriator*, then my loynes were on *Pharoah* and the Egyptians in time of old; you shall weep and howl for the miseries that are suddenly coming upon you; for your riches are corrupted, &c. and whilst impropriated, appropriated the plague of God is in them.

5. The plague of God is in your purses, barns, houses, horses, murrain will take your hogs, O (ye fat swine of the earth) who shall shortly go to the knife, and be hung up i'th roof, except ---- blasting, mill-dew, locusts, caterpillars, yea fire your houses and goods, take your corn and fruit, the moth your garments, and the rot your sheep, did you not see my hand, this last year, stretched out?

You did not see.

My hand is stretched out still.

Your gold and silver, though you can't see it, is cankered, the rust of them is a witnesse against you, and suddainly, suddainly, suddainly, because by the eternall God, my self, its the dreadful day of Judgement, saith the Lord, shall eat your flesh as it were fire, *Jam.* 5. 1. to 7.

The rust of your silver, I say, shall eat your flesh as it were fire.

6. As sure as it did mine the very next day after *Michael* the Arch-Angel's, that mighty Angel, who just now fights that terrible battell in heaven with the great Dragon.

And is come upon the earth also, to rip up the hearts of all bag-bearing Judasses. On this day purses shall be cut, guts let out, men stabb'd to the heart, womens bellies ript up, specially gammer Demases, who have forsaken us, and imbraced this wicked world, and married *Alexander* the Coppersmith, who hath done me much evill. The Lord reward him, I wish him hugely well, as he did me, on the next day after *Michael* the Arch-Angel.

Which was the Lords day I am sure on't, look in your Almanacks, you shall find it was the Lords day, or els I would you could; when you must, when you see it, you will find the Dominicall letter to be G. and there are many words that begin with G. at this time [GIVE] begins with G. give, give, give, give up, give up your houses, horses, goods, gold, Lands,

give

give up, account nothing your own, have ALL THINGS common, or els the plague of God will rot and consume all that you have.

By God, by my self, saith the Lord, its true.

Come! give all to the poore and follow me, and you shall have treasure in heaven. Follow me, who was numbred among transgressors, and whose visage was more marr'd 'then any mans, follow me.

CHAP. III.

A strange, yet most true story: under which is couched that Lion, whose roaring shall make all the beasts of the field tremble, and all the Kingdoms of the earth quake. Wherein also (in part) the subtilty of the wel-favoured Harlot is discovered, and her flesh burning with that fire, which shall burne down all Churches, except that of the first Born, &c.

1. Follow me, who, last Lords day Septem. 30. 1649. met him in open field, a most strange deformed man, clad with patcht clouts: who looking wishly on me, mine eye pittied him; and my heart, or the day of the Lord, which burned as an oven in me, set my tongue on flame to speak to him, as followeth.

2. How now friend, art thou poore?

He answered, yea Master very poore.

Whereupon my bowels trembled within me, and quivering fell upon the worm-eaten chest, [my corps I mean] that I could not hold a joynt still.

And my great love within me, (who is the great God within that chest, or corps) was burning hot toward him; and made the lock-hole of the chest, to wit, the mouth of the corps, again to open: Thus.

Art poor?

Yea, very poor, said he.

Whereupon the strange woman who, flattereth with her lips, and is subtill of heart, said within me,

It's a poor wretch, give him two-pence.

But

But my EXCELLENCY and MAIESTY (in me) scorn'd her words, confounded her language; and kickt her out of his presence.

3. But immediately the WEL-FAVOURED HARLOT [whom I carried not upon my horse behind me] but who rose up in me, said :

, Its a poor wretch give him 6. d. and that's enough for a
, Squire or Knight, to give to one poor body.
, Besides [faith the holy Scripturian Whore] hee's worse
, then an Infidell that provides not for his own Family.
, True love begins at home, &c.
, Thou, and thy Family are fed, as the young ravens strangely,
, though thou hast been a constant Preacher, yet thou hast abhorred both tythes and hire ; and thou knowest not aforehand
, who will give thee the worth of a penny.
, Have a care of the main chance.

4. And thus she flattereth with her lips, and her words being smoother then oile ; and her lips dropping as the honey comb, I was fired to hasten my hand into my pocket; and pulling out a shilling, said to the poor wretch, give me six pence, heer's a shilling for thee.

He answered, I cannot, I have never a penny.

Whereupon I said, I would fain have given thee something if thou couldst have changed my money.

Then faith he, God blesse you.

Whereupon with much reluctancy, with much love, and with amazement [of the right stamp] I turned my horse head from him, riding away. But a while after I was turned back [being advised by my Demilance] to wish him cal for six pence, which I would leave at the next Town at ones house, which I thought he might know [*Saphira* like] keeping back part.

But [as God judged me] I, as she, was struck down dead.

And behold the plague of God fell into my pocket; and the rest of my silver rose up in judgement against me, and consumed my flesh as with fire: so that I, and my money perisht with me

I being cast into that lake of fire and brimstone.

And all the money I had about me to a penny [though I thought through the instigation of my *quondam Mistris* to have reserved some, having rode about 8. miles, not eating one

mouth-

one mouth-full of bread that day, and had drunk but one small draught of drink; and had between 8. or 9. miles more to ride, ere I came to my journeys end: my horse being lame, the waies dirty, it raining all the way, and I not knowing what extraordinary occasion I might have for money.] Yet [I say] the rust of my silver did so rise up in judgement against me, and burnt my flesh like fire: and the 5. of *James* thundered such an alarm in mine ears, that I was fain to cast all I had into the hands of him, whose visage was more marr'd then any mans that ever I saw.

This is a true story, most true in the history.

Its true also in the mystery.

And there are deep ones coucht under it, for its a shadow of various, glorious, [though strange] good things to come.

7. Wel! to return ---- after I had thrown my rusty canker'd money into the poor wretches hands, I rode away from him, being filled with trembling, joy, and amazement, feeling the sparkles of a great glory arising up from under these ashes.

After this, I was made [by that divine power which dwelleth in this Ark, or chest] to turn my horse head ---- whereupon I beheld this poor deformed wretch, looking earnestly after me: and upon that, was made to put off my hat, and bow to him seven times, and was [at that strange posture] filled with trembling and amazement, some sparkles of glory arising up also from under this; as also from under these ashes, yet I rode back once more to the poor wretch, saying, because I am a King, I have done this, but you need not tell any one.

The day's our own.

This was done on the last LORDS DAY, Septem. 30. in the year 1649. which is the year of the Lords recompences for Zion, and the day of his vengeance, the dreadfull day of Judgement. But I have done [for the present] with this story, for it is the later end of the year 1649.

CHAP.

Chap. IV.

How the Author hath been set as a signe and a wonder, as well as most of the Prophets formerly. As also what strange postures the divine Majesty that dwells in his forme, hath set the forme in, with the most strange and various effects thereof upon the Spectators. Also his Communion with the spirits of just men made perfect, and with God the Judge of all, hinted at.

1. IT is written in your Bibles, Behold I and the children whom the Lord hath given me, are for signs and for wonders in Israel, from the Lord of Hoasts, which dwelleth in Mount Sion, *Isa.* 8. 18.

And amongst those who were set thus, *Ezekiel* seems to be higher then the rest by the shoulders upwards, and was more seraphicall then his Predecessors, yet he was the son of *Buzi* (*Ezek.* 1.) which being interpreted is the son of contempt; it pleases me [right well] that I am his brother, a sonne of *Buzi*.

2. He saw [and I in him see] various strange visions; and he was, and I am set in severall strange postures.

Amongst many of his pranks ----- this was one, he shaves all the hair off his head: and off his beard, then weighs them in a pair of scales; burns one part of them in the fire, another part hee smites about with a knife, another part thereof he scatters in the wind, and a few he binds up in his skirts, &c. and this not in a corner, or in a chamber, but in the midst of the streets of the great City Hierusalem, and the man all this while neither mad nor drunke, &c. *Ezek.* 5. 1. 2. 3, 4. &c. as also in severall other Chapt. amongst the rest, Chap. 12. 3. &c. Chap. 4. 3. Chap. 24. 3. to the end. This *Ezekiel* [to whose spirit I am come, and to an innumerable company of Angels, and to God the Judge of all.]

3. [I say] this great Courtier, in the high Court of the highest heavens, is the son of *Buzi*, a child of contempt on earth, and set as a sign and wonder (as was *Hosea*, who went in to a whore, &c.) *Hos.* 2. when he (I say) was playing some of his pranks, the people said to him, wilt thou not tell us what these things are

are to us, that thou dost so, *Ezek.* 24. 19. with the 3. verse and so forwards, when he was strangely acted by that omnipotency dwelling in him; and by that eternall, immortall, INVISIBLE (indeed) Majesty, the onely wise God, who dwells in this visible forme, the writer of this Roule, [who to his joy] is numbred amongst transgressors.

4. The same most excellent Majesty (in this forme) hath set the Forme in many strange Postures lately, to the joy and refreshment of some, both acquaintances and strangers, to the wonderment and amazement of others, to the terrour and affrightment of others; and to the great torment of the chiefest of the Sects of Professours; who have gone about to shake off their plagues if they could, some by crying out he's mad, he's drunk, he's faln from grace, and some by scandalising, &c. and onely one, whom I was told of, by threats of caneing or cudgelling, who meeting me full with face, was ashamed and afraid to look on me, &c.

5. But to wave all this.

Because the Sun begins to peep out, and its a good while past day-break, I'l creep forth (a little) into the mystery of the former history, and into the in-side of that strange out-side businesse.

CHAP.

Chap. V.

The Authors strange and lofty carriage towards great ones, and his most lowly carriage towards Beggars, Rogues, and Gypseys: together with a large declaration what glory shall rise up from under all this ashes. The most strange, secret, terrible, yet most glorious design of God, in choosing base things to confound things that are. And how. A most terrible vial powred out upon the well-favour'd Harlot, and how the Lord is bringing into contempt not only honorable persons, with a vengeance, but all honorable, holy things also. Wholsome advice, with a terrible threat to the Formalists. How base things have confounded base things; and how base things have been a fiery Chariot to mount the Author up into divine glory, &c. And how his wife is, and his life is in, that beauty which makes all visible beauty seem meer deformity.

1. ANd because I am found of those that sought me not. And because some say, wilt thou not tell us what these things are to us, that thou dost so?
Wherefore waving my charging so many Coaches, so many hundreds of men and women of the greater rank, in the open streets, with my hand stretched out, my hat cock't up, staring on them as if I would look thorough them, gnashing with my teeth at some of them, and day and night with a huge loud voice proclaiming the day of the Lord throughout London and Southwark, and leaving divers other exploits, &c. It is my good will and pleasure [only] to single out the former story with its Parallels.

2. [*Viz.*] in clipping, hugging, imbracing, kissing a poore deformed wretch in London, who had no more nose on his face, then I have on the back of my hand, [but only two little holes in the place where the nose uses to stand.]
And no more eyes to be seen then on the back of my hand, and afterwards running back to him in a strange manner, with

my money giving it to him, to the joy of some, to the afrightment and wonderment of other Spectators.

3. As also in falling down flat upon the ground before rogues, beggars, cripples, halt, maimed, blind, &c. kissing the feet of many, rising up againe, and giving them money, &c. Besides that notorious businesse with the Gypseys and Goal-birds (mine own brethren and sisters, flesh of my flesh, and as good as the greatest Lord in England) at the prison in Southwark neer S. Georges Church.

Now that which rises up from under all this heap of ashes, will fire both heaven and earth; the one's ashamed, and blushes already, the other reels to and fro, like a drunken man.

4. Wherefore thus saith the Lord, Hear O heavens, and hearken O earth, Ile overturne, overturne, overturne, I am now stining the pride of all glory, and bringing into contempt all the honourable of the earth, Esa. 23. 9. not only honourable persons, (who shall come down with a vengeance, if they bow not to universall love the eternall God, whose service is perfect freedome) but honorable things, as Elderships, Pastorships, Fellowships, Churches, Ordinances, Prayers, &c. Holinesses, Righteousnesses, Religions of all sorts, of the highest strains; yea, Mysterians, and Spirituallists, who scorne carnall Ordinances, &c.

I am about my act, my strange act, my worke, my strange work, that weosoever hears of it, both his ears shall tingle.

5. I am confounding, plaguing, tormenting nice, demure, barren *Mical*, with *Davids* unseemly carriage, by skipping, leaping, dancing, like one of the fools, vile, base fellowes, shamelessely, basely, and uncovered too, before handmaids,——

Which thing was S. Pauls Tutor, or else it prompted him to write, God hath chosen B A S E things, and things that are despised, to confound——the things are.——

Well! family duties are no base things, they ar things that A R E: Churches, Ordinances, &c, are no B A S E things, though indded Presbyterian Churches begun to live i'th womb, but died there, and rot and stink there to the death of the mother and child. Amen. Not by the Devill, but [by * God] it's true.

* That's a base thing.

Grace

Grace before meat and after meat, are no BASE things; these are things that ARE. But how long Lord, holy and true, &c.

Fasting for strife and debate, and to smite with the fist of wickednesse,---(and not for taking off heavy burthens, breaking every yoke, *Esa.*58.) and Thanksgiving daies for killing of men for money, are no BASE things, these are things that ARE.

☞ Starting up into the notion of spirituals, scorning History, speaking nothing but Mystery, crying down carnall ordinances, &c. is a fine thing among many, it's no base thing (now adaies) though it be a cloak for covetousnesse, yea, though it be to maintain pride and pomp; these are no base things.

6. These are things that ARE, and must be confounded by BASE things, which *S. Paul* saith, not God hath connived at, winked at, permitted, tolerated, but God hath CHOSEN &c. BASE things.

What base things? Why *Mical* took *David* for a base fellow, and thought he had chosen BASE things, in dancing shamelesly uncovered before handmaids.

And barren, demure *Mical* thinks (for I know her heart saith the Lord) that I chose base things when I sate downe, and eat and drank around on the ground with Gypseys, and clip't, hug'd and kiss'd them, putting my hand in their bosomes, loving the she-Gipsies dearly. O base! saith mincing *Mical*, the least spark of modesty would be as red as crimson or scarlet, to hear this.

I warrant me, *Mical* could better have borne this, if I had done it to Ladies: so I can for a need, if it be my will, and that in the height of honor and majesty, without sin. But at that time when I was hugging the Gipsies, I abhorred the thoughts of Ladies, their beauty could not bewitch mine eyes, or snare my lips, or intangle my hands in their bosomes; yet I can if it be my will, kisse and hug Ladies, and love my neighbours wife as my selfe, without sin.

7. But thou Precisian, by what name or title soever dignified, or distinguished, do but blow a kisse to thy neighbours wife, or dare to think of darting one glance of one of thine eyes towards her, if thou dar'st.

It's

It's meat and drink to an Angel [who knows none evill, no sin] to sweare a full mouth'd oath, *Rev.* 10. 6. It's joy to *Nehemiah* to come in like a mad-man, and pluck folkes hair off their heads, and curse like a devill---and make them swear by God,--- *Nehem.* 13. Do thou O holy man [who knowest evill] lift up thy finger against a Jew, a Church-member, cal thy brother fool, and wish a peace-cods on him; or swear I faith, if thou dar'st, if thou dost, thou shalt howl in hell for it, and I will laugh at thy calamity, &c.

8. But once more hear O heavens, hearken O earth, Thus saith the Lord, I have chosen such base things, to confound things that are, that the ears of those [who scorn to be below Independents, yea the ears of many who scorn to be so low as carnall Ordinances, &c.] that hear thereof shall tingle.

9. Hear one word more [whom it hitteth it hitteth] give over thy base nasty stinking, formall grace before meat, and after meat [I call it so, though thou hast rebaptized it---] give over thy stinking family duties, and thy Gospell Ordinances as thou callest them; for under them all there lies snapping, snarling, biting, besides covetousnesse, horrid hypocrisie, envy, malice, evill surmising.

10. Give over, give over, or if nothing els will do it, I'l at a time, when thou least of all thinkest of it, make thine own child the fruit of thy loines, in whom thy soul delighted, lie with a whore---before thine eyes: That that plaguy holinesse and righteousnesse of thine might be confounded by that base thing. And thou be plagued back again into thy mothers womb, the womb of eternity: That thou maist become a little child, and let the mother *Eternity, Almightinesse*, who is universall love, and whose service is perfect freedome, dresse thee, and undresse thee, swadle, unswadle, bind, loose, lay thee down, take thee up, &c.

--- And to such a little child, undressing is as good as dressing, foul cloaths, as good as fair cloaths--- he knows no evill, &c.-- And shall see evill no more,--- but he must first lose all his righteousnesse, every bit of his holinesse, and every crum of his Religion, and be plagued, and confounded [by base things] into nothing.

By base things which God and I have chosen.

11. And

11. And yet I shew you a more excellent way, when you have paſt this. --- In a word, my plaguy, filthy, naſty holineſſe hath been confounded by baſe things. And then [behold I ſhew you a myſtery, and put forth a riddle to you] by baſe things, baſe things ſo called have been confounded alſo; and thereby have I been confounded into eternall Majeſty, unſpeakable glory, my life, my ſelf.

12. Ther's my riddle, but becauſe neither all the Lords of the Philiſtins, no nor my Delilah her ſelf can read it,

I'l read it my ſelf, I'l [only] hint it thus.

Kiſſes are numbered amongſt tranſgreſſors --- baſe things--- well! by baſe helliſh ſwearing, and curſing, [as I have accounted it in the time of my fleſhly holineſſe] and by baſe impudent kiſſes [as I then accounted them] my plaguy holineſſe hath been confounded, and thrown into the lake of fire and brimſtone.

And then again, by wanton kiſſes, kiſſing hath been confounded; and externall kiſſes, have been made the fiery chariots, to mount me ſwiftly into the boſom of him whom my ſoul loves, [his excellent Majeſty, the King of glory.]

Where I have been, where I have been, where I have been, hug'd, imbrac't, and kiſt with the kiſſes of his mouth, whoſe loves are better then wine, and have been utterly overcome therewith, beyond expreſſion, beyond admiration.

13. Again, Luſt is numbered amongſt tranſgreſſors --- a baſe thing.---

Now faire objects attract Spectators eyes.

And beauty is the father of luſt or love.

Well! I have gone along the ſtreets impregnant with that child [luſt] which a particular beauty had begot: but coming to the place, where I expected to have been delivered, I have providentially met there a company of devills in appearance, though Angels with golden vialls, in reality, powring out full vialls, of ſuch odious abominable words, that are not lawfull to be uttered.

Words enough to deafen the ears of plaguy holineſſe. And ſuch horrid abominable actions, the ſight whereof were enough to put out holy mans eyes, and to ſtrike him ſtark dead, &c.

Theſe

These base things (I say) words and actions, have confounded and plagued to death, the child in the womb that I was so big of.

14. And by, and through these BASE things [as upon the wings of the wind] have I been carried up into the arms of my love, which is invisible glory, eternall Majesty, purity it self, unspotted beauty, even that beauty which maketh all other beauty but meer uglinesse, when set against it, &c.

Yea, could you imagine that the quintessence of all visible beauty, should be extracted and made up into one huge beauty, it would appear to be meer deformity to that beauty, which through BASE things I have been lifted up into.

VVhich transcendent, unspeakable, unspotted beauty, is my crown and joy, my life and love: and though I have chosen, and cannot be without BASE things, to confound some in mercy, some in judgment, Though also I have concubines without number, which I cannot be without, yet this is my spouse, my love, my dove, my fair one.

Now I proceed to that which followes.

Chap. VI.

Great ones must bow to the poorest peasants, or els they must rue for it.

No materiall sword, or humane power whatsoever, but the pure spirit of universall Love, which is the eternall God, can break the neck of tyranny, oppression, abominable pride, and cruell murder. A Catalogue of severall judgements recited --- as so many warning-pieces to Appropriators, Impropriators, and anti-free-communicants, &c. The strongest, yea purest propriety that may plead most priviledge shall suddainly be confounded.

1, Again, thus saith the Lord, I in thee, who am eternall Majesty, bowed down thy form, to deformity.

And I in thee, who am durable riches, commanded thy perishable silver to the poore, &c.

Thus saith the Lord,

Kings,

Kings, Princes, Lords, great ones, must bow to the poorest Peasants; rich men must stoop to poor rogues, or else they'l rue for it.

This must be done two waies.

You shall have one short dark hint.

Will. Sedgewick [in me] bowed to that poor deformed ragged wretch, that he might inrich him, in impoverishing himself.

He shall gaine him, and be no great loser himself, &c.

2. Well! we must all bow, and bow, &c. And Meum must be converted.----It is but yet a very little while; and you shall not say that ought that you possesse is your own,&c. read *Act.* 2. towards the end, chap. 4. 31. to the end, with chap. 5. 1. 2. to the 12.

It's but yet a little while, and the strongest, yea, the seemingly purest propriety, which may mostly plead priviledge and Prerogative from Scripture, and carnall reason; shall be confounded and plagued into community and universality. And ther's a most glorious designe in it: and equality, community, and universall love; shall be in requeft to the utter confounding of abominable pride, murther, hypocrisie, tyranny and oppression, &c. The necks whereof can never be chopt off, or these villaines ever hang'd up, or cut off by materiall sword, by humane might, power, or strength, but by the pure spirit of universall love, who is the God whom all the world [of Papists, Protestants, Presbyterians, Independents, Spirituall Notionists, &c.) ignorantly worship.

3. The time is coming, yea now is, that you shall not dare to say, your silver or gold is your owne.

It's the Lords.

You shall not say it is your own, least the rust thereof rise up in judgement against you, and burn your flesh as it were fire.

Neither shall you dare to say, your oxe, or your asse is your own.

It's the Lords.

And if the Lord have need of an asse he shall have him.

Or if two of his Disciples should come to unloose him, I wil not [for a 1000. worlds] call them thieves, least the asse should flat my braines out, my bread is not mine own, it's the Lords.

C   And

> *A rogo, to ask.

And if a poor *Rogue should ask for it — the Lord hath need of it — he should have it, least it should stick in my throat and choak me one way or other.

4. Once more, Impropriators! Appropriators! go to, weep and howl, &c. *Jam.* 5. 1. to the 7. the rust of your silver shall rise (is rising up) against you, burning your flesh as it were fire, &c.

That is (in a word) a secret, yet sharp, terrible, unexpected, and unsupportable plague, is rising up from under all, that you call your own, when you go to count your money, you shall verily think the Devill stands behind you, to tear you in pieces: You shall not put bread in your mouthes, but the curse shall come along with it, and choak you one way or other. All your former sweets shall be mingled with gall and wormwood: I give you but a hint.

It's the last daies.

5. Well! do what you will or can, know you have been warned. It is not for nothing, that I the Lord with a strong wind cut off (as with a sickle) the fullest, fairest ears of corn this harvest, and drop't them on purpose for the poore, who had as much right to them, as those that (impudently and wickedly, theevishly and hoggishly) stile themselves the owners of the Land.

6. It's not for nothing that such various strange kinds of worms, grubs, and caterpillars (my strong host, saith the Lord of Hosts) have been sent into some graine: Neither is in vain, that I the Lord sent the rot among so many sheep this last yeer; if they had been resign'd to me, and you had kept a true communion, they had not been given up to that plague.

7. It's not in vain that so many towns and houses have been lately fired over the heads of the Inhabitants: Neither is it in vain, that I the Lord fired the barning and ricks of a Miser in Worcestershire (this yeer) the very same day that he brought in his own, as he accounted it.

On the very same day (I say) his barning and ricks were fired down to the very ground, though multitudes of very expert men in the imployment came to quench it.

Of this the writer of this Scroule was an eye-witnesse.

8. Impropriators! Appropriators! Misers! a fair warning:
More

More of you shall be served with the same sawce.

Others of you I'le deal withall in another way more terrible then this, faith the Lord, till you resign.----

Misers! specially you holy Scripturian Misers, when you would say grace before and after meat, read *James* 5. 1. to 7. & *Hosea* 2. 8, 9, 10.

Chap. VII.

A further discovery of the subtilty of the wel-favour'd Harlot, with a Parley between her and the Spirit: As also the horrid villany (that lies hid under her smooth words, in pleading against the Letter and History, and for the Spirit and Mystery, and all for her owne ends) detected. Also upon what account the Spirit is put, and upon what account the Letter. Also what the true Communion, and what the true breaking of bread is.

1. BUt now me thinks (by this time) I see a brisk, spruce, neat, self-seeking, fine finiking fellow, (who scornes to be either Papist, Protestant, Presbyterian, Independent, or Anabaptist) I mean the Man of Sin, who worketh with all deceiveablenesse of unrighteousnesse, 2 *Thes.* 2.

Crying down * carnall ordinances, and crying up † the Spirit: cunningly seeking and setting up himself thereby.

* Downe they must, but no thanks to him.
† Up it must, but no thanks to him.

I say, I see him, and have ript up the very secrets of his heart (saith the Lord) as also of that mother of mischief, that wel-favour'd Harlot, who both agree in one, and say on this wise to me.

2. 'Ah! poor deluded man, thou hast spoken of the Wisdome
'of God in a mystery, and thou hast seen all the history of the
'Bible mysteriz'd.

'O fool! who hath bewitcht thee, art thou so foolish as to
'begin in the Spirit, and wilt thou now be made perfect in the
'flesh? keep thee to the spirit, go not back to the letter, keep
'thee to the mystery, go not back to the history.

'What? why dost talk so much of *James* 5. and *Hosea* 2.
'those words are to be taken in the Mystery, not in the History:
'They

'They are to be taken in the Spirit, not as they ise in the Letter.

Thus you have a hint of the neat young mans, and of the well-favour'd Harlots language.

3. But now behold I am filled with the Holy Ghost, and am resolv'd [*Acts* 13.8,9,&c.] to set mine eyes on her and him, (who are no more twaine, but one) and say:

'O full of all subtilty and mischief, thou child of the Devil, 'thou enemy of all righteousnesse, wilt thou not cease to per-'vert the right ways of the Lord?

'Be it known to thee, ô thou deceitfull tongue, that I have 'begun in the spirit, and will end in the spirit: I am joyn'd to 'the Lord, and am one spirit. The spirit's my joy, my life, my 'strength; I will not let it go, it's my delight.

'The mystery is mine, [mostly] that which I most delight in, 'that's the Jewel. The historie's mine also, that's the Cabinet. 'For the Jewels sake I wil not leave the Cabinet, though indeed 'it's nothing to me, but when thou for thine own ends, stand'st 'in competition with me for it.

'Strength is mine, so is weaknesse also.

4. I came by water and blood, not by blood only, but by blood and water also.

The inwardnesse is mostly mine, my prime delight is there; the outwardnesse is mine also, when thou for thine own ends, standest in competition with me about it, or when I would confound thee by it.

5. I know there's no Communion to the Communion of Saints, to the inward communion, to communion with the spirits of just men made perfect, and with God the Judge of all.

No other Communion of Saints do I know.

And this is Blood-life-spirit-communion.

6. But another Communion also do I know, which is water, and but water, which I will not be without: My spirit dwells with God, the Judge of all, dwells in him, sups with him, in him, feeds on him, with him, in him. My humanity shall dwell with, sup with, eat with humanity; and why not [for a need] with Publicans and Harlots? Why should I turne away mine eyes from mine own flesh? Why should I not break my bread to the hungry, whoever they be? It is written, the Lord takes care of Oxen.

And

And when I am at home, I take a great care of my horse, to feed him, dresse him, water him and provide for him.

And is not poor *Meal* of Dedington, and the worst rogue in Newgate, or the arrantest thief or cut-purse farre better, then a 100. Oxen, or a 1000. such horses as mine?

7. Do I take care of my horse, and doth the Lord take care of oxen?

And shall I hear poor rogues in Newgate, Ludgate, cry *bread, bread, bread, for the Lords sake*; and shall I not pitty them, and relieve them?

Howl, howl, ye nobles, howl honourable, howl ye rich men for the miseries that are coming upon you.

For our parts, we that hear the APOSTLE preach, will also have all things common; neither will we call any thing that we have our own.

Do you [if you please] till the plague of God rot and consume what you have.

We will not, wee'l eat our bread together in singlenesse of heart, wee'l break bread from house to house.

CHAP. VIII.

The wel-favoured Harlots cloaths stript off, her nakednesse uncovered, her nose slit, her hunting after the young man, void of understanding, from corner to corner, from Religion to Religion, and the Spirit pursuing, overtaking, and destroying her, with a terrible thunder clap ith' close, &c.

1. ANd we wil strip off thy cloaths, who hast bewitch't us, & slit thy nose thou wel-favoured Harlot, who hast (as in many things, so in this) made the Nations of the earth drunk, with the cup of thy fornications: As thus.

Thou hast come to a poor irreligious wretch, and told him he must be of the same Religion as his neighbours, he must go to Church, hear the Minister, &c. and at least once a year put on his best cloaths, and receive the Communion---he must eat a bit of bread, and drink a sip of wine---and then he hath received, &c. he hath been at the Communion.

2. But when he finds this Religion too course for him, and he would faine make after another,

Then

Then immediately thou huntest after him, following him from street to street, from corner to corner, from grosse Protestantisme to Puritanisme, &c. at length from crosse in baptisme, and Common-Prayer-Book to Presbyterianisme, where thou tellest him he may break bread, with all such believers, who believe their horses and their cowes are their own; and with such believers, who have received different light from, or greater light then themselves; branded with the letter B. banished, or imprisoned fourteen weeks together, without bail or mainprize.

3. And here I could tell a large story, that would reach as far as between Oxonshire and Coventrey.

But though it be in the original copy, yet it is my good will and pleasure, out of my great wisdome, to wave the printing of it, and I will send the contents thereof, as a charge and secret plague, secretly into their breasts, who must be plagued with a vengeance, for their villany against the Lord.

Well! to return from this more then needful digression, to the discovery, and uncovering of the wel-favoured Harlot.

Thou hast hunted the young man void of understanding from corner to corner, from religion to religion.

We left him at the Presbyterian --- where such a believer, who believes his horses and his cows are his own, may have his child christned, and may himself be admitted to the Sacrament ---and come to the communion.

And whats that?

VVhy after a consecration in a new forme, eating a bit of bread, and drinking a sip of wine perhaps once a moneth, why mother of mischief is this Communion?

O thou flattering and deceitfull tongue, God shall root thee out of the Land of the living, is this Communion? no, no, mother of witchcrafts!

5. The true Communion amongst men, is to have all things common, and to call nothing one hath, ones own.

And the true externall breaking of bread, is to eat bread together in singlenesse of heart, and to break thy bread to the hungry, and tell them its their own bread &c. els your Religion is in vain.

6. And by this time indeed thou seest this Religion is in vain.

And

And wilt therefore hie thee to another, to wit, to Independency, and from thence perhaps to Anabaptisme so called.

And thither the wel-favour'd Harlot will follow thee, and say thou must be very holy, very righteous, very religious.

All other Religions are vain.

And all in the Parish, all in the Countrey, yea all in the Kingdome, and all in the world [who are not of thine opinion] are without, are of the world.

Thou, and thy comrades are Saints.

[O proud devill! O devill of devills! O *Belzebub*!]

Well [saith she] thou being a Saint must be very holy, and walk in Gospell-Ordinances [saith the wel favour'd Harlot] ay and in envy, malice, pride, covetousnesse, evill surmising, censoriousnesse, &c. also.

And on the first day of the week, when the Saints meet together, to break bread, do not thou omit it upon pain of damnation.

By no means omit it, because thou hast Gospell Ordinances in the purity of them.

- Papists---they give wafers.---

Protestants---give- -to all ith' Parish ragg ragg, and his fellow if they come.

But we are called out of the world, none shall break bread with us, but our selves, [the Saints together, who are in Gospell Order.]

Besides the Priests of England cut their bread into little square bits, but we break our bread [according to the Apostolicall practise] and this is the right breaking of bread [saith the wel-favour'd Harlot.]

Who hath stept into this holy, righteous Gospell, religious way, [Gospel-Ordinances so called] on purpose to dash to pieces the right breaking of bread: and in the room thereof thrusting in this vain Religion.

7. A Religion wherein *Lucifer* reignes, more then in any.

And next to this in the Independents [so called] both which damn to the pit of hell, those that are a 100. times nearer the Kingdome of heaven then themselves: flattering themselves up in this their vain Religion.

But take this hint before I leave thee.

He that hath this worlds goods, and seeth his brother in want, and shutteth up the bowells of compassion from him, the love of God dwelleth not in him; this mans Religion is in vain.

His Religion is in vain, that seeth his brother in want, &c.

H's brother———a beggar, a lazar, a cripple, yea a cut-purse, a thief ith' goal, &c.

He that seeth such a brother, flesh of his flesh [in want] and shutteth up the bowels of his compassion from him, the love of God dwelleth not in him, his Religion is in vain: and he never yet broke bread————that hath not forgot his [*meum*.]

9. The true breaking of bread————is from house to house, &c. Neighbours [in singlenesse of heart] saying if I have any bread, &c. it's thine, I will not call it mine own, it's common.

These are true Communicants, and this is the true breaking of bread among men.

10. And what the Lords Supper is, none know, but those that are continually [not weekly] but daily at it. And

And what the true Communion is, those and those only know, who are come to the spirits of just men made perfect, and to God the Judge of all, all other Religion is vain.

Ay, saith the wel-favour'd Harlot [in the young man void of understanding] I see Protestantism, Presbytery, Independency, Anabaptism, are all vain. These coverings are too short, too narrow, too course for me; the finest of these are but harden sheets, and very narrow ones also.

I'l get me some flax, and make me both fine and large sheets, &c. I'l scorn carnall Ordinances, and walk in the Spirit.

Ay, do [saith the wel-favour'd Harlot] speak nothing but mystery, drink nothing but wine, but bloud, thou need'st not eat flesh, &c.

12. And so my young man starts up into the notion of spirituals, and wraps up a deal of hipocrisie, malice, envy, deceit, dissimulation, covetousnesse, self-seeking in this fine linnen.

Being a hundred fold worse Devills then before.

But now thy villanie, hipocrisie, and self-seeking is discovering, yea discovered to many with a witnesse.

And though the true and pure levelling, is the eternall Gods levelling the Mountains, &c. in man. Which is the
Bloud-Life-Spirit levelling.

Yet the water, or weak levelling, which is base and foolish, shall confound thee.

And hereby, (as also by severall other strange waies, which thou art least of all acquainted withall. I'l discover thy lewdnesse, and shew the rottennesse of thy heart.

I'l call for all to a mite, to be cast into the outward treasury.

And wil bid thee lay down all at my feet, the Apostle, the Lord, And this is a way that I am now again setting up to try, judge, and damne the wel-favour'd Harlot by.

Cast all into the Treasury, &c. account nothing thine owne, have all things in common.

The young man goes away very sorrowfull, ———— &c.

The wel-favour'd Harlot shrugs at this.————

13. When this cometh to passe, a poore wretch whose very bones are gnawn with hunger, shall not go about 13. or 14. miles about thy businesse, and thou for a reward, when thou hast hundreds lying by thee.

I will give thee but one hint more, and so will leave thee.

The dreadful day of Judgement is stealing on thee, within these few hours. Thou hast secretly and cunningly lien in wait, thou hast craftily numbered me amongst transgressors, who to thy exceeding torment, am indeed a friend of Publicans and Harlots.

Thou hast accounted me a devil, saith the Lord.

And I wil rot thy name, and make it stink above ground, and make thy folly manifest to all men.

And because thou hast judged me, I wil judge thee (with a witnesse) expect it suddainly, saith the Lord.

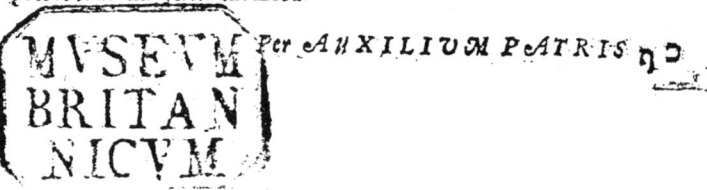

Per AUXILIUM PATRIS